First published in 2022 by
Hungry Tomato Ltd
F1, Old Bakery Studios,
Blewetts Wharf, Malpas Road,
Truro, Cornwall, TR1 1QH, UK

Thanks to our creative team
Senior Editor: Anna Hussey
Graphic Designer: Amy Harvey
Editorial Assistant: Charlotte Moyle

A CIP catalog record for this book is
available from the British Library.

Beetle Books is an imprint of Hungry Tomato.

ISBN 978-1-914087-45-5

Printed and bound in China

Discover more at:
www.mybeetlebooks.com
www.hungrytomato.com

WHAT MACHINES DO

written by John Allan

illustrated by Esther Cuadrado

CONTENTS

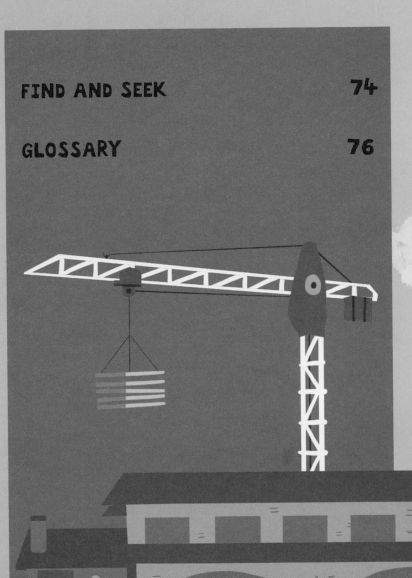

WHAT DO MACHINES DO?

Machines are everywhere! We use them for all sorts of tasks, from baking a cake to flying to the moon. Life would be much harder and less fun without them.

HARD AT WORK

Some machines help us do our jobs, while others get us where we need to go. Machines can help us relax and have fun, and some can even save our lives!

EVERYDAY MACHINES

Have you ever wondered how many machines are in your home? Why don't you try to count them all? It might be more than you think!

ABOUT THIS BOOK

Prepare to visit lots of busy machines doing all sorts of different things. Take a look at them in action and then turn the page to discover what they do and how they work.

ON THE CONSTRUCTION SITE

There is a lot going on at this construction site. Look at the big, heavy machines helping the builders with their work.

ON THE CONSTRUCTION SITE

Bulldozers are used to clear the ground to get it ready for building.

Tracks help it move over muddy and uneven ground.

Bulldozer

Dump trucks are used to carry heavy loads of materials like sand, gravel or soil.

It can lift and tip its box to empty its load.

Dump Truck

Excavators are used to dig up soil from the ground.

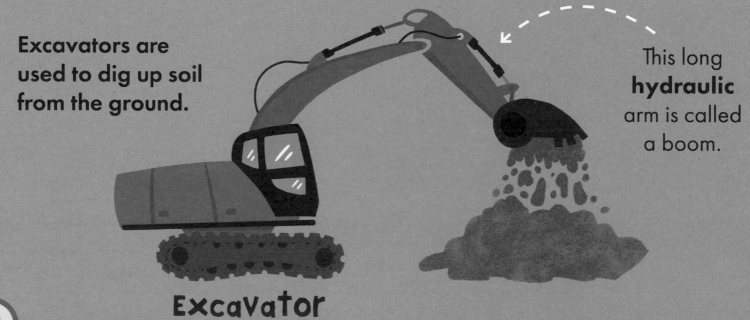

This long **hydraulic** arm is called a boom.

Excavator

These machines are used to drill giant holes.

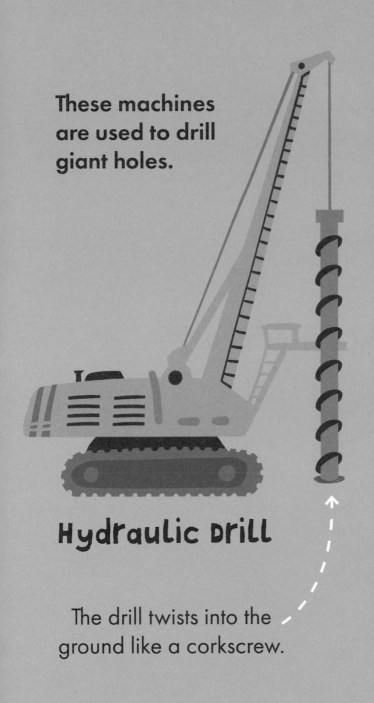

Hydraulic Drill

The drill twists into the ground like a corkscrew.

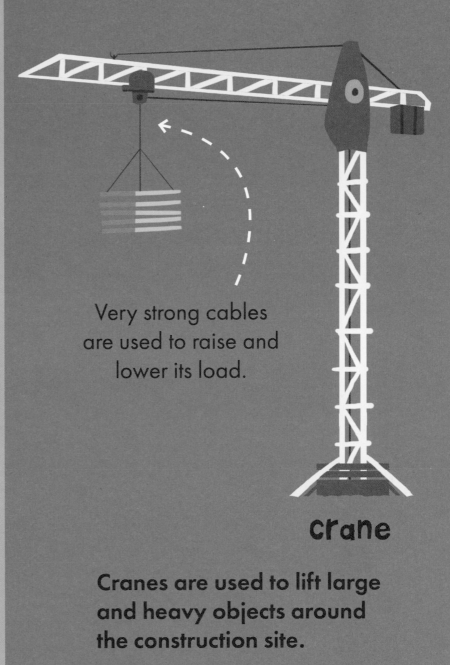

Crane

Very strong cables are used to raise and lower its load.

Cranes are used to lift large and heavy objects around the construction site.

This truck makes concrete by mixing sand, gravel, water and cement in its drum.

Concrete Mixer

This drum turns round and round to mix the concrete.

ON THE FARM

There's lots to do on the farm. Machines can make a farmer's job much easier.

15

ON THE FARM

Tractors do many jobs, including pulling other machines, like ploughs.

They have big, thick wheels for grip in muddy fields.

Tractor

A plough is used to loosen and turn soil before crops are planted.

Blades on the plough dig into the soil.

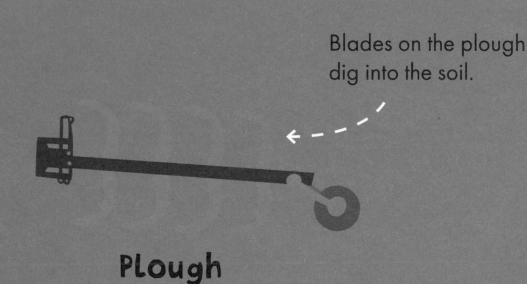

Plough

Combine harvesters are used to cut and harvest crops.

Sharp blades cut the crops, while spinning spikes pull them into the machine.

combine Harvester

This machine is attached to the back of a tractor to plant potatoes.

It drops potatoes into the ground and covers them over with soil.

Potato Planter

This machine is used to milk a cow.

These tubes are attached to a cow's udders to pump milk into a big container.

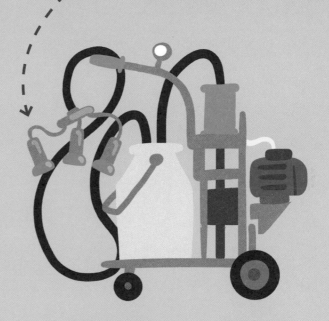

Milking Machine

A baler packs cut hay into **bales** so that it can be easily transported and stored.

Once the machine has made a bale, it drops it out of the back.

Hay Baler

AT THE HOSPITAL

Hospitals have lots of machines and vehicles to help people who are hurt or sick.

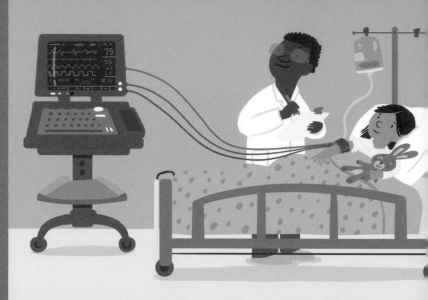

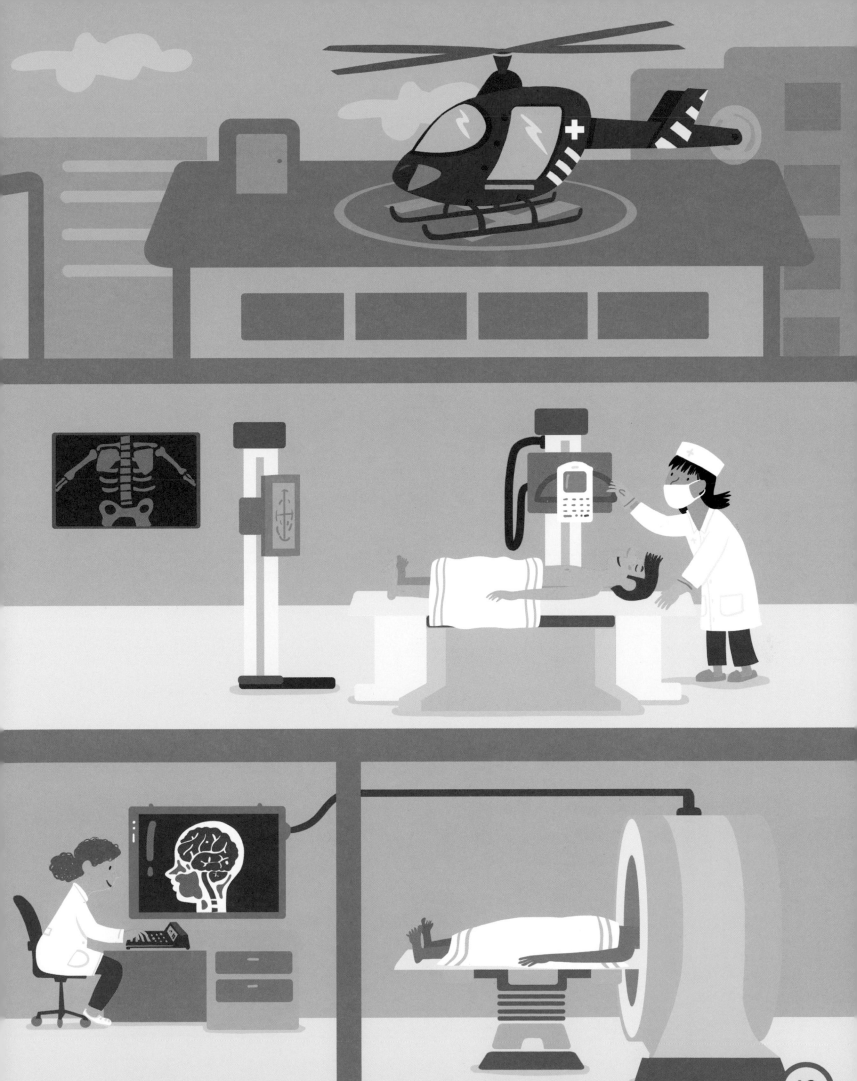

19

AT THE HOSPITAL

An x-ray machine is used to check for broken bones and other illnesses.

It takes a special black and white picture of the inside of your body.

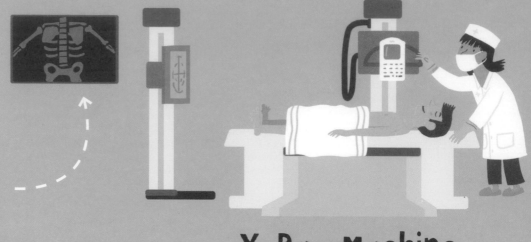

X-Ray Machine

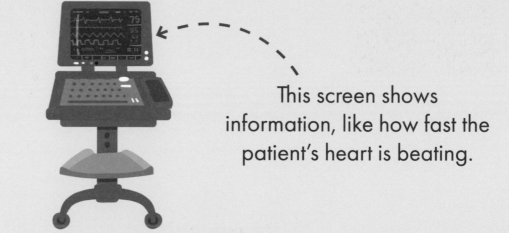

Patients are connected to this machine to keep track of their health.

This screen shows information, like how fast the patient's heart is beating.

Patient Monitor

Doctors use microscopes to hunt for tiny things that can make you sick, like **germs**.

Its **lenses** make things look much bigger when you look through them.

Microscope

An MRI machine takes more detailed pictures than an x-ray. It can even see inside your brain!

The bed moves inside the donut-shaped machine to scan your body.

MRI Machine

These vehicles take sick people to hospital in an emergency.

Inside the back there's lots of equipment to help keep people alive.

Ambulance

This speedy helicopter is used for emergencies that are too difficult to get to in a regular ambulance.

These blades spin round really fast to lift the helicopter into the air.

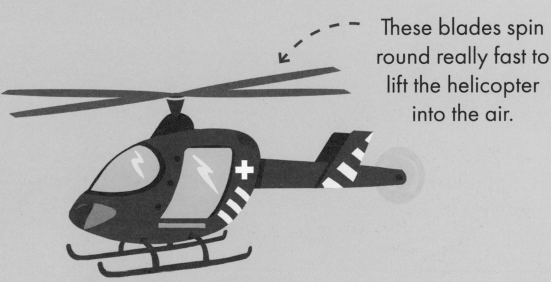

Air Ambulance

ON THE ROAD

Vehicles are machines that we use
to travel around, and our roads
are full of them!

ON THE ROAD

Buses help many people get where they need to go every day.

Buses are long, with lots of seats for passengers.

Bus

Cars are a very popular way to travel. They come in lots of different shapes and sizes.

Cars have headlights so the driver can see where they are going in the dark.

Car

Police cars are used for patrolling and driving to crime scenes.

When there is an emergency, the driver will turn on their flashing lights and a loud **siren**.

Police Car

When a vehicle breaks down on the road, a tow truck may be brought in to help move it.

This arm is called a boom. It lifts vehicles onto the back of the truck.

Tow Truck

A motorcycle has two wheels, like a bicycle, but its **engine** makes it much faster.

Motorcycle riders wear a helmet to keep them safe.

Motorcycle

Trucks transport all kinds of things. They often travel very long distances with heavy loads.

Trucks use a lot of **fuel**, so they have big tanks to keep them going.

Trucks

AT THE AMUSEMENT PARK

A trip to an amusement park can be a fun day out! There are lots of different rides to try out.

AT THE AMUSEMENT PARK

Roller coasters are the biggest and fastest rides at the park.

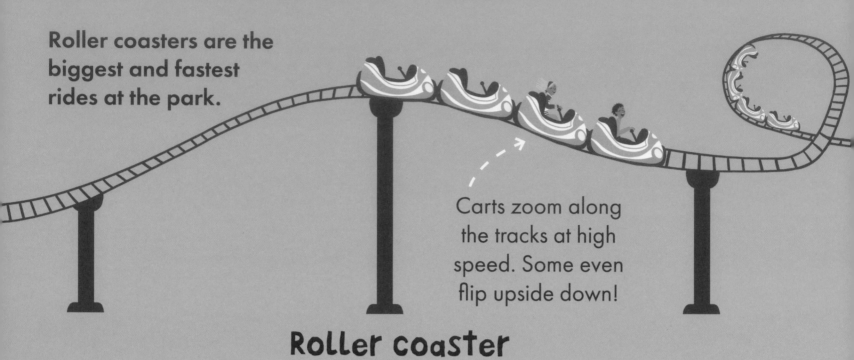

Carts zoom along the tracks at high speed. Some even flip upside down!

Roller coaster

This ride could make you very dizzy!

People sit inside teacups that spin round faster and faster!

Teacup Ride

These are little cars that you drive round a ring, trying to avoid the other cars.

Each car has a rubber edge that bounces off other cars.

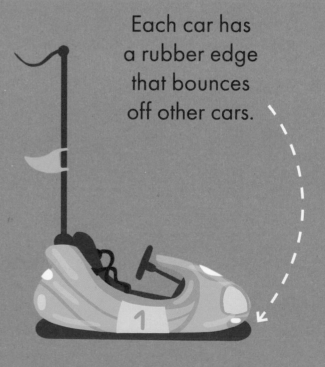

Bumper cars

Merry-go-rounds play music as you go up and down, and round and round.

The horses move up and down, while the whole ride spins in a circle.

Merry-go-round

You can see for miles from the top of a Ferris wheel!

People sit in these cabins as the wheel spins round slowly.

Ferris Wheel

Prepare for a splash on this water ride.

Boats fall down a steep waterfall into a pool of water.

Log Flume

AT HOME

Some machines around the home are used to keep things clean and tidy, while others are just for fun!

AT HOME

Radiators are used to warm up your house when it's cold.

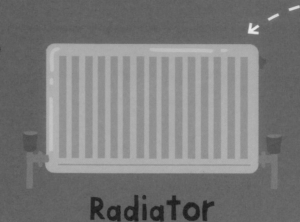

There are different kinds of radiator. This one is full of water, which heats up.

Radiator

A lawn mower is used to cut grass.

Inside, an engine spins a blade that cuts through grass as it is pushed along.

Lawn Mower

This is used to clean up dirt and dust from around the house.

Dirt is sucked up through this tube into a bag or container inside the machine.

Vacuum Cleaner

A television, or TV, is a screen for watching movies or shows, or for playing video games on.

You can control what is shown on the TV using a **remote control**.

Television

An iron is used to smooth out wrinkles from clothes and other fabrics.

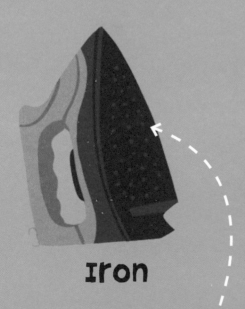

Iron

The metal plate gets very hot and steam comes out of the holes. Never touch it when it's on!

This machine is used to wash your clothes.

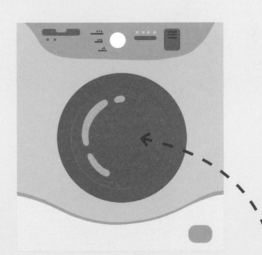

Washing Machine

The hole inside is called a drum. It fills with water and soap, and spins round to clean your clothes.

AT THE AIRPORT

Off on a trip? How many machines will you see on your journey through the airport?

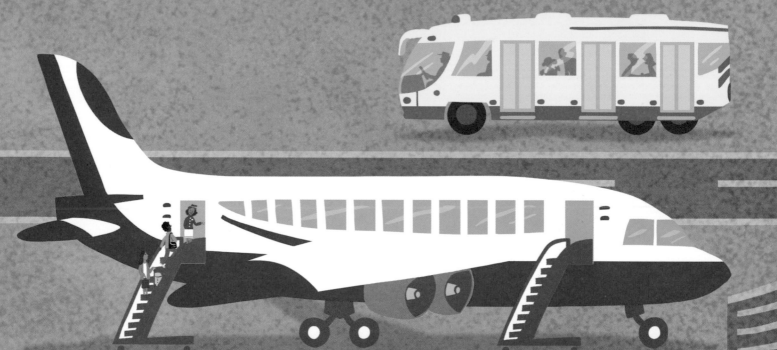

AT THE AIRPORT

Fuel trucks transport fuel to planes so that they can be refilled between flights.

Fuel stored in this large tank gets pumped into the planes through a hose.

Fuel Truck

Shuttle buses carry passengers and crew to and from their plane.

Electric doors make it easy for passengers to get on and off.

Shuttle Bus

These are used to load and unload baggage from planes.

This ramp helps lift baggage up into the **cargo hold** of the plane.

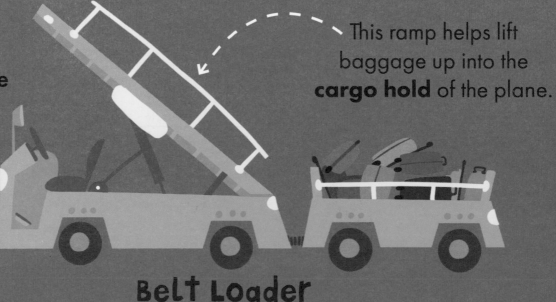

Belt Loader

An airliner is a plane that carries lots of passengers. They fly all over the world.

Inside the front of the plane is the cockpit. It is full of controls that the pilot uses to fly the plane.

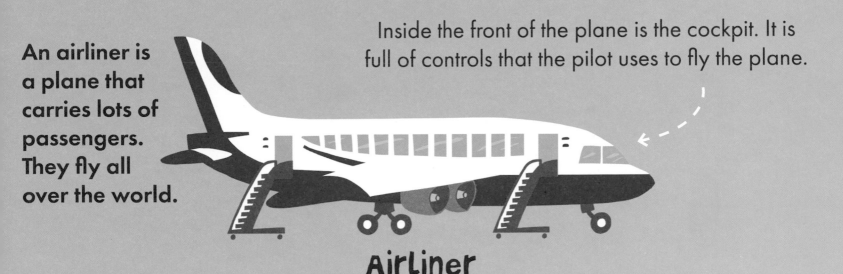

Airliner

This machine is used to check baggage for items that aren't allowed on planes.

This screen shows an **x-ray image** of the baggage in the machine.

Baggage X-ray Machine

People arriving at the airport after a flight collect their baggage here.

The **conveyor belt** moves along, carrying baggage around until its owner collects it.

Baggage Carousel

AT THE AUTO-REPAIR SHOP

Mechanics have lots of special tools and machines to fix cars and other vehicles.

AT THE AUTO-REPAIR SHOP

An engine hoist is used to lift a heavy engine out of a car.

Pumping this lever moves the arm up or down.

Engine Hoist

This lifts a vehicle off the ground so mechanics can get underneath to work on it.

Vehicle Lift

These controls move the lift up and down.

This machine checks a wheel is balanced, so that it spins smoothly.

A wheel is attached here, and the machine spins it round.

Wheel Balancer

An oil drainer is used to remove old oil from a vehicle, so that it can be replaced.

This machine can recharge or kickstart a car battery.

These clips are used to attach the battery to the machine.

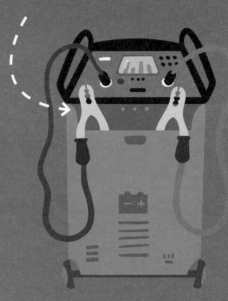

The old oil collects in this tank.

Oil Drainer

Battery Charger

A spray gun is used to give cars a new coat of paint.

When the trigger is pulled, the machine sprays paint evenly onto the car.

Spray Gun

41

ON THE STREET

The more you look around you on the street, the more machines you'll see!

ON THE STREET

These trucks rush firefighters to a fire and help them put it out.

Water sprays out of this hose to put out a fire.

Fire Engine

These lights tell **pedestrians** whether to stop or go at a street crossing.

When the walking person is lit up, it's safe to cross the road.

Pedestrian Signal

These machines are often found in walls on the street. It is like a mini **bank**.

ATM Cash Machine

You can use it to take out cash from your bank account. The money comes out from this slot.

Bicycles are a fun way to travel and get some exercise.

Bicycle

Peddles powered by your feet make the wheels turn.

Street sweepers keep our roads and streets clean.

Brushes at the front spin round, sweeping up trash and leaves.

Street Sweeper

This vehicle collects trash from our homes and towns.

The back has a special crusher to squish down trash that is thrown into it.

Garbage Truck

AT THE GROCERY STORE

There are lots of machines at work in the grocery store. Some are keeping food fresh, while others help you shop.

AT THE GROCERY STORE

Freezers are very cold inside! Frozen foods can stay fresh much longer than food in a fridge.

They keep some frozen foods, like ice cream, from melting.

Freezer

A floor polisher is pushed around to keep the floor in the store clean and shiny.

The brush on the bottom spins to collect dirt and polish the floor.

Floor Polisher

You put fruit and vegetables on these scales to find out how much they cost.

Produce Scales

It prints a label so the **cashier** will know how much you need to pay.

A cash register scans the items you're buying and tells you and the cashier how much you need to pay.

This little box can print you a **receipt** once you've paid.

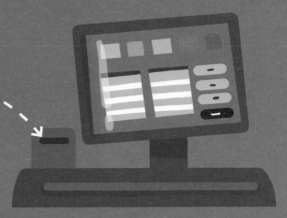

Cash Register

This counter is used to display foods like cooked meats and cheeses, and keep them fresh and cool.

The glass case lets customers see the food, while keeping it clean.

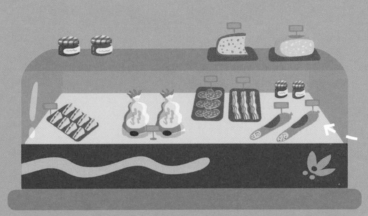

Deli Counter

You put the things you are ready to purchase on this machine.

The top is a conveyor belt that carries your items towards the cashier.

Checkout Conveyor

AT A ROCKET LAUNCH

Prepare for liftoff! It takes a lot of different machines to send a **spacecraft** up into space.

AT A ROCKET LAUNCH

Rockets send spacecraft into space. Different parts perform separate tasks during a launch.

In outerspace, the spacecraft is released from the rest of the rocket, to travel on its own.

Spacecraft

This is the part that astronauts travel in.

This is the largest part of the rocket. It provides most of the power to shoot the spacecraft into space.

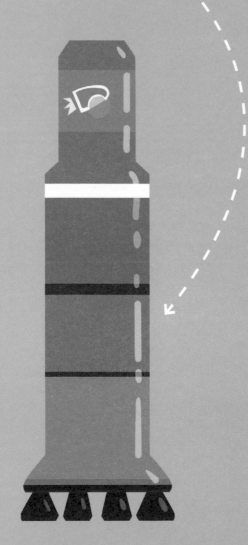

Rocket Propulsion System

Rocket boosters give an extra push during liftoff.

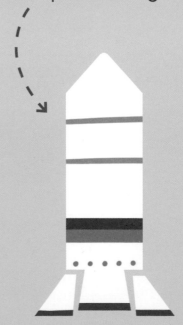

Rocket Boosters

These metal towers are arranged around the **launchpad** to stop **lightning** striking the rocket.

They're much taller than the rocket, so any lightning should strike them instead.

Lightning Protection Tower

This tower supports the rocket while it is being built and transported.

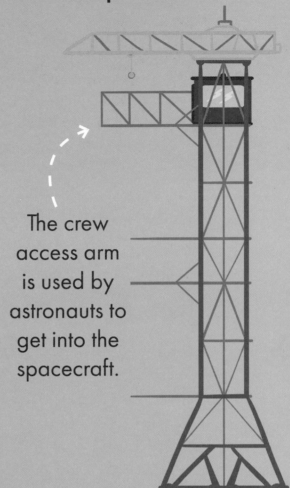

The crew access arm is used by astronauts to get into the spacecraft.

Mobile Launcher

This enormous vehicle carries rockets and spacecraft to their launchpad.

It has four tracks that move it along very slowly.

Crawler Transporter

AT THE ARCADE

There are lots of fun games to play at the arcade, and they all work in different ways.

AT THE ARCADE

Two players follow the dance moves on the screen to see who's the best dancer.

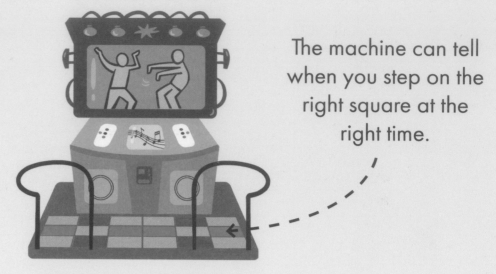

The machine can tell when you step on the right square at the right time.

Dance Machine

This game can make it feel like you're riding a real motorcycle!

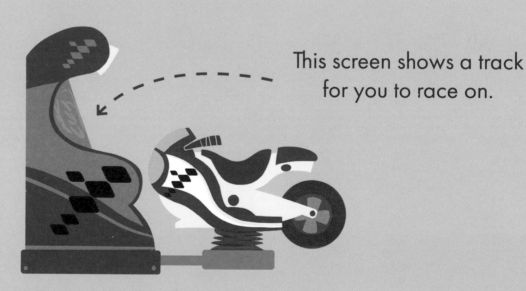

This screen shows a track for you to race on.

Motorcycle Simulator

There are lots of different types of video games, with different aims and rules.

They all have a screen to show the game, and controls to play it.

Arcade Video Game

This game tests your strength.

Boxing Machine

Punch this bag really hard to try and beat the highest score.

Win a prize by catching it in the claw.

Claw Machine

These controls move the claw around and tell it when to grab.

The aim of this game is to knock over all the bowling pins with a ball.

New balls are released here.

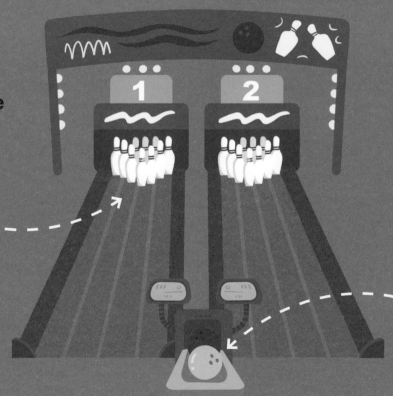

Bowling Alley

AT A ROADWORKS SITE

Have you ever thought about how roads get made? It takes a lot of machines.

59

AT A ROADWORKS SITE

Graders are used to flatten out the ground before the new road surface is put down.

Road Grader

This blade scrapes along the ground, dragging away loose dirt and stones.

A paver spreads a layer of **asphalt** onto the ground to make a new road surface.

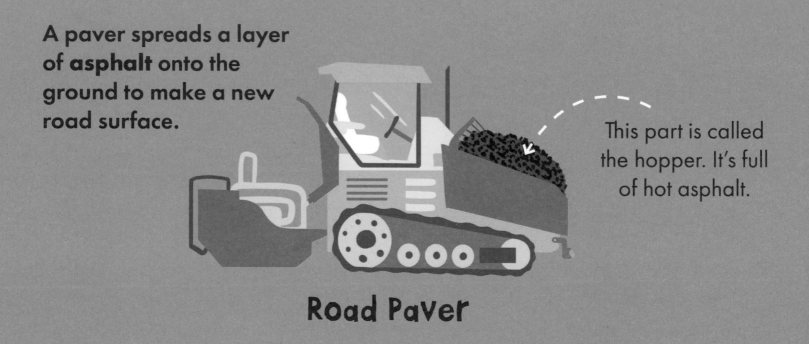

Road Paver

This part is called the hopper. It's full of hot asphalt.

A road roller is used to flatten down the new asphalt.

Instead of wheels, it has very heavy rollers.

Road Roller

A milling machine removes old road surfaces, so that they can be replaced.

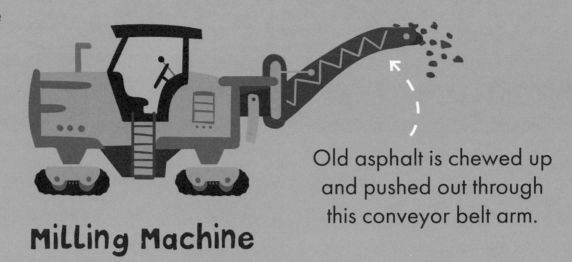

Milling Machine

Old asphalt is chewed up and pushed out through this conveyor belt arm.

Also called a jackhammer, this drill breaks through hard surfaces, like concrete.

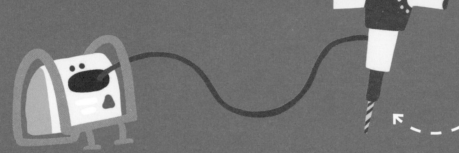

Pneumatic Drill

It moves up and down very fast and hammers the ground hard to break it up.

This is used to paint **road markings** on a new road.

Paint comes out here as the machine is pushed along, leaving a smooth line.

Road Marking Machine

AT THE COFFEE SHOP

At this coffee shop, lots of tasty drinks and treats are made using machines.

AT THE COFFEE SHOP

This oven is used for baking tasty cakes and pastries.

A grill heats up sandwiches and makes them nice and crispy.

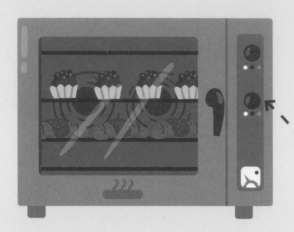

Pastry Oven

Inside the oven can get very hot. These dials are used to set the perfect temperature.

Sandwich Grill

Closing the lid presses two hot **grills** onto the top and bottom of the sandwich to heat it.

This machine can make different types of coffee.

This spout blows hot steam into milk to make it hot and frothy.

Coffee Machine

64

Dishwashers clean dirty plates, cups, glasses, and cutlery.

Dirty dishes are stored in trays inside the machine, ready to be washed.

Dishwasher

This grinds coffee beans into a powder to make coffee with.

The beans are poured into the top of the machine.

Coffee Grinder

Blenders are used to make drinks like milkshakes and smoothies.

Blender

Spinning blades at the bottom of the jug turn fruit and other ingredients to liquid.

AT THE TRAIN STATION

Trains aren't the only machines at this station. Even the clock is helping people catch their trains on time.

AT THE TRAIN STATION

These gates stop people getting onto **railway platforms** without a ticket.

When you scan or insert your ticket, the doors open to let you through.

Ticket Barriers

Trains travel on tracks instead of roads. Some trains travel very long distances.

They are split into **coaches** that connect to each other. Trains with lots of coaches can be very long!

Train

You can use this machine to buy a ticket for your train journey.

Once you've paid, the machine prints your ticket, and it comes out here.

Ticket Machine

Lights like this tell the train driver when to stop or go.

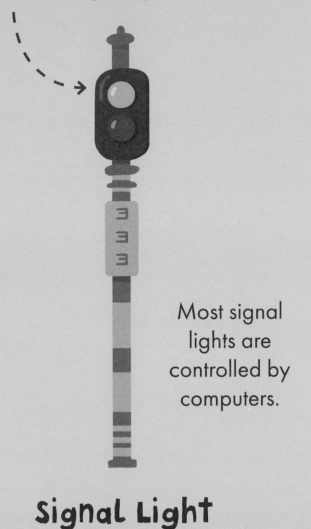

Most signal lights are controlled by computers.

Signal Light

Many train stations have vending machines so you can buy drinks or snacks for your journey.

You use these buttons to select what you want to buy.

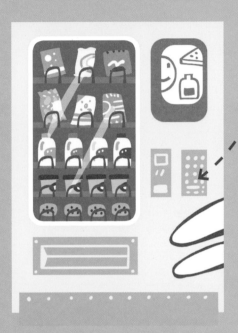

Vending Machine

An escalator is a moving staircase, powered by a motor.

People carefully step onto the moving stairs to travel up or down.

Escalator

AT THE BEACH

Nothing beats a sunny day at the beach! There are lots of brilliant boats and other machines to spot.

AT THE BEACH

This boat is powered by a motor. It can travel very fast.

It has a steering wheel to change direction.

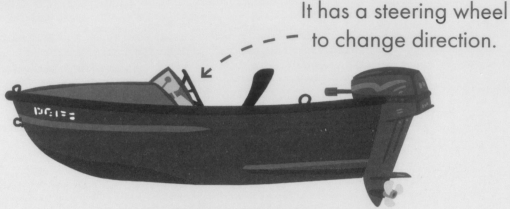

Motor Boat

Lifeboats are used to rescue people at sea.

The doors and windows are tightly sealed so no water can get in during storms.

Lifeboat

These vehicles speed along by pumping powerful jets of water out of the back.

Riders stand or sit on a water scooter, a bit like a motorcycle.

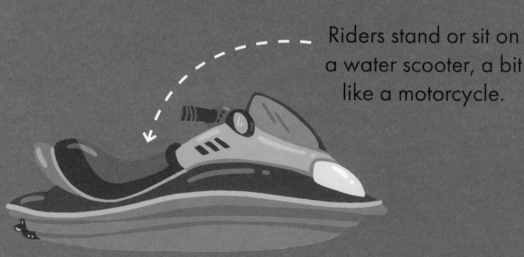

Water Scooter

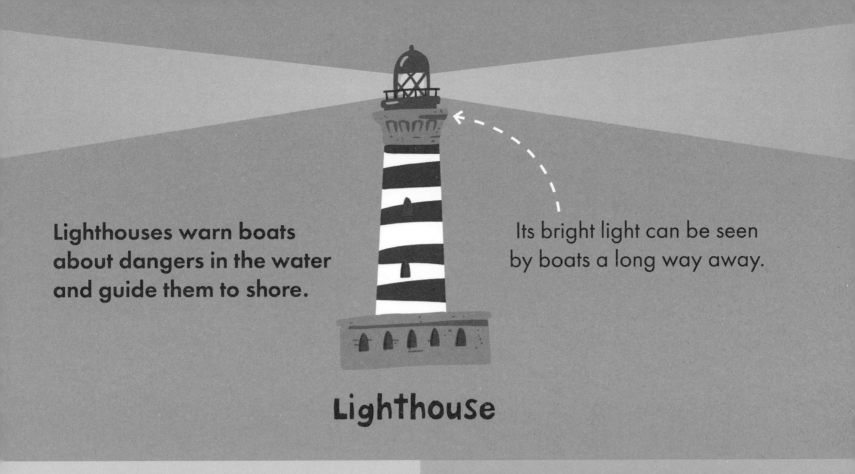

Lighthouses warn boats about dangers in the water and guide them to shore.

Its bright light can be seen by boats a long way away.

Lighthouse

Ice cream can be a refreshing treat on a hot day.

Ice cream cart

This cart has a freezer inside to keep the ice cream frozen.

You can look through these to see far out to sea.

Put a coin in this slot to see through the **binoculars**.

coin Operated Binoculars

FIND AND SEEK!

Can you find which machine each of these pictures are a part of?

1.

CLUE: You might get wet on this ride!

2.

CLUE: This machine has a hose to put out fires.

3.

CLUE: This machine is a game to see who's the best dancer.

4.

CLUE: You put produce on this to find out how much it will cost.

5.

CLUE: This machine is used to cook yummy pastries and cakes.

6.

CLUE: This machine has a freezer inside.

8.

CLUE: Passengers collect their bags from this machine after a flight.

7.

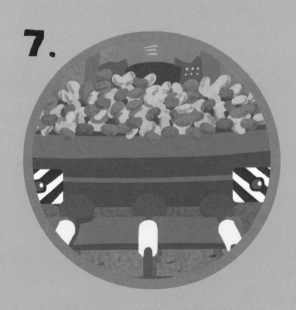

CLUE: This machine plants a particular vegetable on the farm.

DID YOU FIND THEM ALL?

Answers can be found on page 77.

GLOSSARY

Asphalt
A material used to make smooth road surfaces.

Bales
A large bundle of something, such as hay.

Bank
A business where people store their money.

Binoculars
A device that you look through with both eyes to see far away.

Cargo hold
Part of a plane or ship where baggage or goods are stored.

Cashier
A person whose job it is to take money for purchases at a store.

Coaches (train)
Separate sections of a train that connect together.

Conveyor belt
A moving surface used to transport objects from one place to another.

Engine
Part of a machine or vehicle that turns fuel (see below) into energy to make it move.

Fuel
A substance, such as oil or gas, which is used to power a vehicle or other machine.

Germs
Tiny living things that can cause diseases in plants and animals.

Grills
Surfaces that can be heated up to cook food on.

Hydraulic
Something that is moved by a liquid, such as water, being put under pressure.

Launchpad
A platform where rockets are launched from.

Lenses
Clear curved pieces of glass or plastic that can make things look clearer, bigger or smaller, when looked through.

Lightning
Giant electrical sparks that can strike during a storm. It can cause damage to objects that it hits.

Mechanics
A person whose job it is to repair and look after vehicles and machines.

Motor
Part of a machine that makes something move. Similar to an engine (see opposite).

Patients
People being looked after in hospital.

Pedestrians
A person who travels by foot, walking or running.

Railway platforms
An area next to part of a railway track where trains stop so that passengers can get on and off.

Receipt
A piece of paper with information about a purchase you have made.

Remote control
A handheld machine used to operate another machine, such as a television or sound system.

Road markings
Lines, symbols or words painted on roads to give drivers important information.

Siren
A loud warning sound.

Spacecraft
A machine or vehicle designed to travel in outer space.

X-ray image
A special photograph, taken using an x-ray machine, to show inside an object or person.

FIND AND SEEK ANSWERS

ANSWERS: 1. Log flume, 2. Fire truck, 3. Dance machine, 4. Produce scales, 5. Pastry oven, 6. Ice cream cart, 7. Potato planter, 8. Baggage carousel

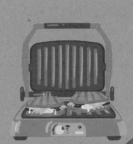

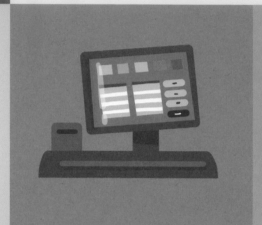

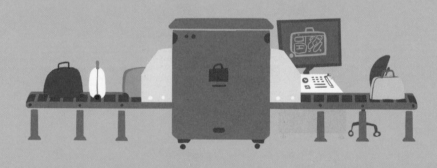

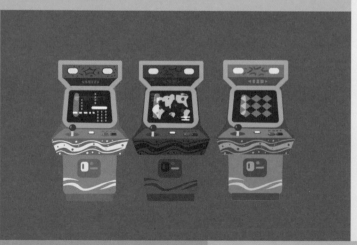